# JOAN OF ARC

## "I'M NOT AFRAID...
## I WAS BORN TO DO THIS"

### PHILIP WILKINSON

# CONTENTS

## THE GIRL FROM DOMRÉMY

Farmer's Daughter 8
Jeannette 10
Pious and Pure 12
The Hundred Years' War 14
Beware Raiders! 16
The Voices 18

## JOAN'S STRUGGLE

The Journey to Chinon 22
Medieval Women 24
Tried and Tested 26
Preparing for Battle 28

# JOAN AT WAR

| | |
|---|---|
| On the March | 32 |
| Medieval Warfare | 34 |
| Victory! | 36 |
| Coronation | 38 |
| Trouble Ahead | 40 |
| Captured | 42 |

**3**

# PRISONER AND MARTYR

**4**

| | |
|---|---|
| In Prison | 46 |
| The Medieval Church | 48 |
| The Trial | 50 |
| Burned at the Stake | 54 |
| Changing their Minds | 56 |
| Joan's Legacy | 58 |
| | |
| Glossary | 60 |
| Bibliography and Index | 62 |

# THE GIRL FROM DOMRÉMY

1

la pucelle

# Farmer's Daughter

Above: This late 14th-century stained-glass window is from a series depicting stories from the Bible. It shows Eve and her baby. Eve is dressed in the kinds of clothes that Isabelle would have worn.

Previous page: This 15th-century book illumination, drawn after Joan's death, shows her dressed as a shepherdess.

Around January 1412, a baby girl was born in the small village of Domrémy in northeastern France. Her parents called her Jeanne, the French form of Joan. They could not have guessed that before her short life was over, she would become famous all over Europe and change the history of her country.

Joan's parents were farmers. Like most country people in the 15th century, they made a living growing crops and raising livestock. Her father, Jacques d'Arc, was not rich, but he was well respected. When his neighbours had a dispute with a local lord, they chose Jacques to plead their case.

Joan's mother was called Isabelle. She was born in a village near Domrémy and, according to one story, she was a devout woman who had been on a long pilgrimage. Going on any long journey was not easy in the Middle Ages. Most people had to walk, the roads were poor and there was the chance of being attacked and robbed. So pilgrims needed to be both determined and brave.

Although Joan's parents were respected in the village, they had little power or influence: politics was the business of lords, kings and churchmen.

## 1337
The Hundred Years' War begins between England and France.

## 26 August 1346
Edward III of England defeats French king Philip VI at the Battle of Crécy, in northern France.

Farmers spent their lives in the fields, and their wives and children helped them.

Jacques and Isabelle had other children as well as Joan. Two older boys, Jacques and Jean, helped on the farm. Another daughter, Catherine, probably died as a child. A third boy, Pierre, was born some time after Joan. As for Joan herself, her parents would have hoped that, like most farmers' daughters, she would find a husband, probably from a local family.

Below: Joan's small stone-built house in Domrémy still stands and is now a museum. When the village became famous as Joan's birthplace, a statue of her was placed above the doorway.

### The Middle Ages

The period between 500 and 1500 is known as the Middle Ages. It was a time when countries were usually ruled by kings or queens. Most people lived in the countryside. Much of the land was owned by the king, who portioned it out to his lords in return for their loyalty. The lords portioned out some of their land to tenants, like Jacques d'Arc. In return, tenants gave the lord a share of the food they produced.

### 1382 onward

France is divided by struggles between the dukes of Orléans and Burgundy.

### January 1412

Joan is born to parents Isabelle and Jacques in the village of Domrémy, in northeastern France.

# Jeannette

Joan spent her early years at her parents' farm in Domrémy. Her family called her Jeannette, an affectionate form of her name normally used for small children. People who knew her as a child said that she was well behaved and popular around the village.

In the 15th century, most children did not go to school. Few people could read or write apart from members of the clergy or boys who were going to have a career in the church. Most other people learned the skills they would need in adult life from their parents. For a young girl like Joan, this meant helping her mother in the house and her father on the farm.

**Below: This group of fighting boys are not misbehaving – they are practising the art of warfare, watched by their teacher. One day they would have to go to war and fight for real.**

## 1413
Henry V becomes king of England and quickly begins to plan new attacks on the French.

## 1415
Czech church leader Jan Hus is called before a church council and is burned at the stake for his beliefs.

## Working children

People in the Middle Ages did not think they were being cruel when they made children work. They thought that it was the best way to train them for adult life. Since most people had to grow their own food, it was also a good way of making sure that everyone had enough to eat. Children had to grow up quickly – many were doing as much work as an adult by the time they were 12 years old.

From Isabelle, Joan would have learned how to cook, do the laundry and keep the house clean and tidy. Since most people had to make their own clothes, she would also have learned how to spin the wool from her father's sheep into thread and how to sew. In addition, Isabelle probably kept a small garden where she would have grown vegetables and herbs for the kitchen.

Medieval women were also expected to help their husbands and fathers in the fields. They might do all sorts of tasks, from ploughing to helping with the harvest. Because Joan had two older brothers, she probably did not need to do too much heavy work. But she did her fair share of taking care of the animals.

Although Joan no doubt had plenty of work to do, there might also have been time for play. There were no elaborate toys. Joan would have been lucky if one of her brothers carved her a doll from a fallen tree branch. But medieval children were good at making toys out of anything they could find lying around. They used cherry pits as marbles, small rocks as counters, or built play houses out of sticks. And Joan might have got together with other children from the village to play games with leather balls. She may even have joined the village boys in the war games they made up.

## 25 October 1415

Henry V's archers score a major victory for England at the Battle of Agincourt in northern France.

## 1417

Martin V is elected pope and puts an end to the Great Schism, or split, that has divided the Catholic Church.

# Pious and Pure

In most ways, young Joan was like all the other children in the village of Domrémy. But one thing made her stand out. In the Middle Ages almost everyone went to church regularly, but Joan was especially religious. She liked to go to church not just on Sundays but whenever she could get away from her duties on the farm.

Joan, like most other children at the time, was baptised by the local parish priest soon after she was born. From that time on, she went to church with her family every Sunday, and on special festivals and saints' days. Joan prayed a lot, was fascinated by the story of Jesus and the lives of the saints, and liked to visit the shrine of the Virgin Mary in the little chapel at the nearby village of Bermont. According to one story, even when she was supposed to be watching her father's cattle in the fields she often secretly walked to Bermont to visit the shrine.

Many of the adult villagers admired Joan's piety. Most people believed in God, so it was seen as a virtue to be devout. Some of Joan's friends, however, teased her about her religion.

## Village customs

The Domrémy children took part in a local custom called 'dancing around the fairy tree'. They danced around a tree, hung garlands of flowers in its branches and hoped to get a glimpse of the fairies. Joan took part in the singing and dancing but was not really interested. Unlike some of the children, she never claimed to have seen a fairy.

## 1417
King Henry V of England continues his advance through France, conquering Normandy.

## 1419
Philip the Good becomes Duke of Burgundy and starts to make his duchy one of Europe's most powerful states.

Most of them would rather be playing outdoors than inside praying to the statue of a saint. But Joan did not seem to mind being teased. This was part of Joan's

**Above: A small group of people have gathered in church in this illustration from a 15th-century book. A priest is blessing one of the congregation.**

character that came out very strongly later – she was not afraid to be different from other people, and was always very sure of her beliefs.

Perhaps Joan's piety was influenced by her mother. Isabelle might have hoped that a sincere belief in God would help her daughter through the difficulties in life faced by most women at this time. Women usually had to marry someone chosen by their parents, and Joan was promised to a young local man when she was still a girl. Married women had few rights compared with their husbands. Even worse, once they began to have children, they faced great dangers. The modern healthcare we enjoy today did not exist, and many women died in childbirth.

**1420**
The Treaty of Troyes brings a brief peace, making Henry V heir to the French king Charles VI.

**1420**
Henry V marries Catherine, daughter of Charles VI, bringing the two countries closer together.

# The Hundred Years' War

In the 14th and 15th centuries, the map of Europe looked different from the way it does today. Parts of eastern France were not ruled by the French king but by the Duke of Burgundy. Areas of western France were ruled by the English, and several English kings, who were related to the French royal family, laid claim to the rest of France, too.

During Joan's lifetime, a long war raged between the French and English over who should control France. The conflict began in 1337, when the English king, Edward III, whose mother was a French princess, declared himself ruler of France in spite of the fact that there was already a French king, Philip VI, on the throne. The war continued on and off until 1453.

In the years before Joan entered the war, the English, under their king Henry V (reigned 1413–22), and their allies the Burgundians, seemed to be gaining the upper hand, especially in battles such as Agincourt (1415). But from 1429 onward, the French forces, partly thanks to Joan, scored major victories, putting most of France back in French hands.

**Above: During the Hundred Years' War, diplomacy was just as important as fighting. The leader of one side would send envoys, or messengers, to meet his opponent and discuss terms. This picture shows King Charles VI of France receiving envoys (kneeling) from England.**

**Right: Battles in the 15th century began in a very formal way, with both sides forming tidy ranks and lining up some distance apart, as shown in this picture of the beginning of the Battle of Agincourt. Each leader tried to find the best place to line up his men. Both foot soldiers and cavalrymen took part in the fighting. Some of the foot soldiers were archers, and they could do great damage before the horsemen began to charge and hand-to-hand fighting began.**

KEY

Approximate area of land controlled by England

Approximate area of land controlled by Burgundy

Approximate area of land controlled by France

The site of a battle of the Hundred Years' War

Thames

London

ENGLAND

Agincourt

Crécy

Beaurevoir

Somme

Beaulieu

NORMANDY

Seine

Oise

Soissons

Rouen

Compiègne

St Denis

Crépy-

Rheims

Paris

en-Valois

Meuse

Formigny

Melun

Vaucouleurs

Domrémy

Neufchâteau

Patay

Troyes

Beaugency

Orléans

Chécy

Tours

Blois

Gien

Auxerre

BURGUNDY

Loire

La Charité

Chinon

Fierbois

Loire

SWITZERLAND

Vienne

Poitiers

FRANCE

Rhône

ITALY

Garonne

Avignon

Right: Toward the end of a battle, as here at Crécy, the opposing sides came together in close combat. Man struggled with man, everyone fighting desperately for their lives. Knights armed with lances and swords clashed with one another and with foot soldiers as the scene became more and more confusing. In the heat of battle, the different heraldic colours and symbols on banners, such as the lions of England and the fleur-de-lis of France, were essential to help distinguish one side from the other.

# Beware Raiders!

Life in a country torn by war is always difficult and dangerous. Although the battles in the Hundred Years' War were separated by long periods without fighting, there were dangers other than battles for the people of France. Domrémy was in territory held by the English when Joan was a girl, so it was especially vulnerable.

At the time of the Hundred Years' War, countries did not have permanent armies made up of professional soldiers as they do today. Neither was there

Above: Men-at-arms could do very well with the booty they collected after a battle. These soldiers are busy counting the gold coins they have found while their comrades and enemies lie dead.

a system for getting food and other supplies to the fighting men. Instead, kings relied on their nobles to supply men-at-arms to fight on their behalf. These men could be unruly and poorly disciplined. Usually they had to get their food from the territory they conquered – and often they had to take what they needed by force.

Sometimes, hungry and bored between battles, the men-at-arms went on a rampage, stealing cattle for food. Often, they did not stop at thieving. To prevent villagers from retaliating, they killed anyone who stood in their way.

**I September 1422**
Henry V dies in France before he can succeed to the French throne.

**21 October 1422**
Charles VI of France dies, leaving his son, Charles the Dauphin, as uncrowned king-in-waiting.

Right: A group of men ransacks a large village house. The men on the left have found a barrel of wine. Another pair are carrying away a chest, which would have contained the occupants' most valuable possessions.

The raiders burned down people's houses and sometimes assaulted the women. An attack from a foreign army could destroy a small village, and France was under threat from two armies – those of England and of Burgundy.

## Men-at-arms

Most fighting men in the 15th century were not sword-wielding knights on horseback but men-at-arms, or foot soldiers. They specialised in different weapons, the most popular being various types of bows, including short continental bows, English longbows and the crossbow, which was more powerful than the other types but took much longer to prepare and load.

In 1425, when Joan was about 13 years old, a band of Burgundians, together with some English, attacked Domrémy. They drove off most of the village cattle, took valuables from the church and set it on fire. It took a lot of hard work by the villagers to fix the damage, and it left them with a hatred of the raiders, especially the Burgundians, who were from eastern France. Joan's only consolation was that her family was safe and she had not been attacked.

## 1422

John, Duke of Bedford, is appointed to rule France and England on behalf of English king Henry VI, who is a baby.

## 1425

A band of Burgundian and English raiders attacks the village of Domrémy, taking cattle and other booty.

# The Voices

In 1425, soon after the raid on Domrémy, something extraordinary began to happen to Joan. She started to hear voices, which seemed to belong to long-dead Christian saints. These voices told Joan what to do, and the more she listened to them, the more she was convinced that she had been given a special task by God.

When Joan first heard the voices, they told her that she should pray and be diligent in going to church regularly and worshipping God. Later, the voices made a much more bizarre request: they instructed her to lead a French army and defeat the English and Burgundians. The rest of Joan's short life would be taken up with following these instructions and coping with the results of her actions.

Today, the story of Joan's voices seems very strange. Why should heavenly saints ask an unknown girl from a remote village to take on a great army? But the Middle Ages was a period when many people had a strong belief in God, and although religious visions were unusual, there were a number of stories of people who had seen or heard saints or angels.

Above: In this painting by the great 15th-century Italian artist Pisanello, St Michael is portrayed as a figure of angelic beauty.

## 1425

Joan begins to hear voices, which she believes to be those of the Saints Catherine, Margaret and Michael.

## May 1428

Joan asks Robert de Baudricourt for help for the first time.

So when Joan talked about the voices, many people did not think she was mentally ill or untruthful, as they might today. They thought this was an example of the powerful ways in which God could make his wishes known on Earth. But some members of the clergy were suspicious. They thought that people should only be able to communicate with God by means of prayers and rituals led by priests.

Above: St Margaret, who was seen as capable of fighting any enemy, is shown in this 14th-century illustration defeating a dragon, a medieval symbol of evil.

Joan came to believe that the voices she heard belonged to St Catherine, St Margaret and St Michael. Both St Catherine and St Margaret were Christian women who were killed because they refused to marry non-Christian men. St Michael, also an angel, was a saint who was said to have led heaven's forces against Satan and who had been chosen by the French army as a patron saint. All were strong, active saints who were prepared to fight for their beliefs, and all were often portrayed holding a sword. They were just the saints to stand by someone who was going to lead an army.

Right: St Catherine died being tortured on a wheel, and she is often shown either holding a wheel or standing on one.

## June 1428

Warned of another attack by raiders, the villagers of Domrémy flee to the fortified town of Neufchâteau for safety.

## August 1428

Joan is summoned to appear in court, accused of breaking a promise to marry a local man. She wins her case.

# JOAN'S STRUGGLE

2

# The Journey to Chinon

**Having heard the voices urging her to fight, Joan had to decide what to do. As a farmer's daughter, she knew nothing of armies or politics, and most people in her position would have ignored the voices. But Joan's determination and deep religious faith made her obey their call.**

Joan knew that if she was to act she would need to meet the French Dauphin, Charles, and ask his permission to lead an army. 'Dauphin' was the name given to the heir to the throne. But after the death of his father in 1422, the French throne had not passed to Charles but to the king's nephew, King Henry VI of England, because of a treaty his father had signed to try to make peace with England. Charles and his followers did not accept the treaty and hoped to win back the throne.

**Previous page: This book illumination shows Joan on horseback and equipped with a banner and armour.**

**Below: The town of Chinon still has its medieval walls and fortress, standing on a rise above the Vienne River. The fortifications have been rebuilt and extended several times, but Joan would have seen many of these walls when she visited the town.**

## January–February 1429
Joan again visits Robert de Baudricourt at Vaucouleurs to ask for his support for her mission.

## 22 February 1429
Joan leaves the town of Vaucouleurs and starts her journey to Chinon.

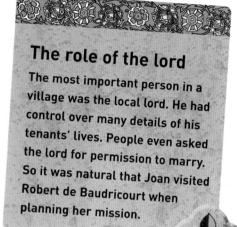

Left: German tapestry-makers of the 15th century produced this image of Joan arriving at the gates of Chinon. The city walls, towers and drawbridge are all visible, but in real life Charles did not stand on the drawbridge to welcome her.

### The role of the lord

The most important person in a village was the local lord. He had control over many details of his tenants' lives. People even asked the lord for permission to marry. So it was natural that Joan visited Robert de Baudricourt when planning her mission.

In May 1428, when Joan was probably 16 years old, she went to visit the most powerful local lord, Robert de Baudricourt, and asked him to help her meet Charles. But Baudricourt thought her mission was ridiculous and sent her home.

Joan's voices continued to urge her on. In early 1429, Charles and his court were at the castle of Chinon, about 220 miles (350 kilometres) from Domrémy. Joan decided she must visit him there, but had no way of making this long journey quickly or safely. She had no horse and no men to protect her. So she asked Baudricourt for help again. Some of his knights were inspired by her story, and decided that they would go with her if their lord would give permission. Finally, Baudricourt decided he should support her.

So on 22 February 1429, Joan and a band of followers began their two-week journey to Chinon. By the time they arrived, news of Joan's mission had reached Charles, and he wanted to find out whether she was a true visionary – and a genuine ally.

**February–March 1429**
Joan and her followers stop off at enemy-held towns as they make their way toward Chinon.

**4 March 1429**
Joan arrives at the castle of Chinon and waits to see the Dauphin.

# Medieval Women

In the Middle Ages, women had less power and fewer rights than men. Most married, and were expected to provide support to their husbands and to raise a family. Women had little choice about the lives they led, but there were a few areas in which they could make their mark. Some women became nuns, and some nuns rose to positions of power as abbesses, like the famous 12th-century abbess Hildegard of Bingen. She communicated with popes and kings, and wrote music that is still performed today. Some middle-class women occasionally became traders. Widows sometimes found it possible to lead a more independent life, too. But it was very rare for a woman to put on armour and go into battle – and especially rare to take a leading role.

**Left: Fifteenth-century women spent most of their time working in and around the house. One of the most important activities was spinning – taking sheep's wool and turning it into thread that could then be woven into cloth to make clothes. All women learned to spin, even people like this French woman who, judging by her comfortable-looking house, was probably wealthy.**

**Below: Many women helped in the fields, often doing quite heavy work, especially at busy times such as harvest. These French women from the time of Joan of Arc are getting in the hay harvest. Joan herself would probably have taken part in tasks like this.**

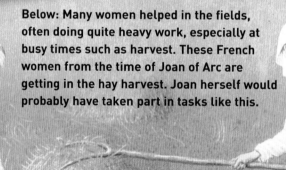

Right: Women who became nuns dedicated their entire lives to the service of God. When entering the convent, they promised to leave behind their worldly possessions, to give up contact with the opposite sex and to obey the head of the convent at all times. The figure on the right of this picture is a nun taking these vows of poverty, chastity and obedience. From then on most of her life would be devoted to prayer and religious observance, though she would also learn how to read and perhaps how to write, and could acquire other skills, such as nursing the sick.

## A FAMOUS WRITER

Few women outside the convents learned to read or write, but one famous woman who did was Christine de Pisan (1363–1430). Christine was born in France and was alive at the same time as Joan. She became famous as one of the greatest poets of her time. Her works included love poems, a biography of the French king Charles V and an educational book for women. Christine also wrote in praise of Joan's military successes.

# Tried and Tested

Because Joan had the support of Robert de Baudricourt, a powerful lord, she was quickly allowed into the castle of Chinon to see the Dauphin. But many people at the royal court were still suspicious of Joan, so they thought up a trick to test her.

Joan was admitted to the great hall of the castle where the court – about 300 people – was assembled. At the centre of the crowd was a man wearing prince's clothes bearing the fleur-de-lis, the symbol of the French royal family. But this was not the Dauphin. Charles stood to one side, pretending to be an ordinary nobleman. Quickly, Joan ignored the man who was dressed as Charles and made her way across to the real Dauphin and kneeled at his feet. She had never seen Charles before.

Many were deeply impressed by the way Joan singled out Charles. Joan also seemed to have a good effect on Charles.

**Left: The church of Notre Dame de la Grande at Poitiers was already very old when Joan went to the town in 1429. The west front was built by the finest artists and masons of the 12th century.**

## 6 March 1429

Joan is received by the Dauphin Charles at the castle of Chinon.

## 10 March 1429

Joan is questioned at Chinon about the reasons for her actions.

She was able to cheer up this moody and indecisive man. But others feared that Joan's seemingly magical abilities and her voices might be the work of the devil. So Charles sent her to Poitiers, where various senior churchmen gathered to interview her.

The records of Joan's interview have been lost, but she must have impressed the churchmen. They probably approved of her for another reason, too. Joan's appearance seemed to be fufilling an old prophecy that a maiden would come to save France.

When the priests said Joan's instructions had indeed come from God, many people were convinced. However, it was extremely unusual for a woman to lead an army. There are a few records of medieval queens leading troops into battle, but a peasant girl had never been put in this position before. As incredible as it seems, Charles and his courtiers sent Joan away to prepare for battle.

### The power of prophecy

Priests in the Middle Ages were impressed by any event that had been predicted. Christians see the birth of Jesus as fulfilling a prediction in the Old Testament. So when Joan's actions seemed to mirror an old prophecy, it was easy to think that God had sent her.

Above: St Francis of Assisi was the founder of the order of friars known as the Franciscans. As part of their investigations into Joan, church authorities sent friars to Domrémy to find out about her background.

**11 March 1429**
Joan travels to the town of Poitiers, where she is further questioned by a jury of churchmen.

**24 March 1429**
Joan returns to the castle of Chinon and prepares for battle.

# Preparing for Battle

Joan now had the approval of both Charles and the churchmen, and she was at last able to prepare for the military campaign that would lead to a French victory and open the way for Charles to be crowned king of France. The next step was for Joan to travel to the city of Tours on the Loire River, where an armourer was waiting to make her a suit of armour.

Plate armour, made up of sheets of metal joined together with leather straps, had to be custom made, so that it protected the body while allowing freedom of movement. In early April 1429, Joan was measured for her armour. When the suit was finished it was uncomfortable at first. But the plates moved easily when she walked and Joan soon got used to it.

For most of the rest of her life Joan would wear armour and male clothes. This shocked many people because she was rejecting the traditional behaviour of a medieval woman. But Joan did not care what her critics said.

At the same time, Joan gathered the other equipment she would need. She ordered a standard and some banners.

Left: Charles, shown in later life in this portrait by the painter Jean Fouquet, was impressed with Joan. Once she had the backing of the church he allowed her to take her place as a military leader.

### 2 April 1429

A horseman is sent to find Joan's sword in the church of St Catherine at Fierbois.

### 4 April 1429

Joan and her followers prepare to leave Chinon.

She also needed a sword. Joan insisted that the sword she should carry was hidden behind the altar of a church, St Catherine's at Fierbois. She said that the voices had told her about it, although it is possible that Joan had seen the sword during one of her visits to the church. When men were sent to find it, the sword was just where she had said.

By now Joan had a large following among the French men-at-arms. The men were unruly and swore a lot. Joan urged them to behave themselves, and she soon had one of the most disciplined armies of the time behind her. As they marched out of Tours, they were well prepared for battle.

## Banners and symbols

In the Middle Ages, banners on the battlefield bore the coat of arms of the owner so that soldiers could see which side people were on. But Joan's banners were different. They bore images of Jesus and of angels, and the phrase 'De par le Roi de Ciel' (On the side of the King of Heaven).

Below: The castle of Chinon was one of the homes of the kings of France and so was both large and well fortified. It now houses a museum dedicated to Joan's life.

**5 April 1429**
Joan sets out from Chinon and begins her journey to the city of Tours.

**11 April 1429**
Joan arrives in Tours and orders her armour, standard and other equipment for battle.

# JOAN AT
# WAR

3

# On the March

Joan was convinced that she should help one of the most important of all French cities, Orléans, which had been besieged, or surrounded, by the English for six months. So she and her army began a long march, northeastward, roughly along the line of the Loire River, to the great city.

By now, Joan had gathered around her a force of about 4,000 men. She must have felt strange as a totally untrained woman leading such a large force. But her faith in the voices must have given her strength.

Even though the journey was long, Joan travelled with the soldiers, never asked for extra comforts and quickly won the men's respect. Charles had appointed a man called Jean d'Aulon to be her steward and bodyguard, and he rode at her side, as did two of her brothers, Pierre and Jean.

Joan was also given two pages to help her and two heralds, a special honour and a sign that Charles regarded her very highly. Heralds carried messages from one commander to another and wore a special uniform so that they did not get attacked.

Above: Most noblemen in Joan's time could not read or write. They each carried a seal, with a unique design, with which to stamp their letters instead of signing them. This seal belonged to Jean, Count of Dunois. He was the illegitimate son of the Duke of Orléans.

Previous page: Joan is seen dressed in armour and wielding a sword and banner in this illumination from a 15th-century French manuscript.

**21 April 1429**
Joan leaves Tours on her next journey: a march along the Loire Valley toward Blois.

**25 April 1429**
Joan and her men arrive in Blois, where they prepare for the final stage of their march to Orléans.

In late April 1429, as Joan's army came within a few miles of Orléans, it met up with Jean, Count of Dunois. Jean, known as the Bastard of Orléans because he had been an illegitimate child, was in charge of defending the city, and told Joan how things stood.

In the early 15th century, Orléans had a population of about 30,000 – a large city by the standards of the time. It was surrounded by a stone wall with towers and some 21 cannons pointing at anyone trying to force their way in. The English had cannons, too, but they could not blow a hole in the city's thick walls. So they camped outside the gates, preventing anyone from coming out, and hoping that Orléans would run out of food and surrender.

**Right: Many of the houses in France in Joan's lifetime were built with a wooden framework. The house in Orléans where Joan stayed was built in this way and was reconstructed in the 20th century.**

## Walled cities

Cities in the Middle Ages had many houses belonging to wealthy merchants and lords. To make them safe in times of war, cities were protected by strong stone walls. The gateways in the walls were heavily fortified, and defenders could spot any possible attacks from watchtowers.

### 29 April 1429

Joan arrives at Chécy, to the east of Orléans. In the evening she enters Orléans by the Burgundy Gate.

### 1 May 1429

Joan remains in Orléans while the Count of Dunois goes to Blois to find the rest of the French army.

# Medieval Warfare

Most of the conflicts that Joan was involved in were sieges, rather than pitched battles. In a siege, an attacking army surrounded a walled city or castle and tried to get inside and take over. Sometimes they did this by smashing down the walls or gates using battering rams or catapults. Or they might attempt to climb over the walls using ladders. But in some cases the attacking army simply surrounded the walls so that no one could get out, and waited until the city ran out of food. Meanwhile, those inside the walls occasionally dashed out to make a lightning attack on the besiegers.

Below: A siege tower could be wheeled up to a castle wall. It had a roof to protect the attackers from arrows and a platform from which the besiegers could jump into the attack. But because many castles had moats or ditches it was often not possible to use siege towers.

Above: The attackers might try climbing up ladders placed against the walls. The problem with this was that the climbers became easy targets for archers on the castle's battlements, so the attackers also had to keep up a steady rain of arrows on the defenders. Even then, a defender might still be able to push away the ladders.

Left: Besiegers often used big wooden catapults, called trebuchets, to hurl heavy stones at the defenders. The stones would injure defenders and knock holes in the walls. The besiegers seen here are about to use their trebuchet to hurl a rock. When the big weight is released, the sling will fly through the air and hurl the rock toward the tower.

Right: Instead of climbing the walls, attackers often tried to break them down by mining – digging a tunnel under the moat, walls and foundations of the castle so that a stretch of wall collapsed. The attackers built a wooden shed to protect the miners from enemy fire. Often, the defenders would throw flaming torches on to the shed to try to destroy it. Clever miners put damp animal hides on the roof of the shed, to protect it from fire.

# Victory!

When she arrived outside the city of Orléans, Joan wanted to fight right away. But Count Jean de Dunois, the defender of Orléans, was more concerned with getting food supplies into his besieged city. He also knew that, if Joan could somehow enter the city before fighting, her presence would give its people more enthusiasm to fight the English.

Count Jean's thinking shows how the French leaders viewed Joan. They thought of her as a figurehead, someone who could inspire the troops with her charisma, while the commanders actually took charge of the fighting.

Joan's first triumph was to enter the city unharmed by slipping in through an unguarded gate along with a few followers. As Count Jean had predicted, her arrival lifted the spirits of the citizens and everyone looked forward eagerly to the moment when they could mount an attack on the English.

The first opportunity came a few days later, on 4 May, when a skirmish broke out at St Loup, a monastery near the city's eastern side. Joan, angered that Count Jean had not bothered to tell her, quickly put on her armour and rode out toward the action.

**Right: In the Middle Ages many of those wounded in battle did not survive. This illustration shows a doctor examining a urine sample to work out what is wrong with a wounded soldier.**

## 4 May 1429

Joan takes the fortified monastery of St Loup, her first victory at Orléans.

## 5 May 1429

On Ascension Day there is no fighting. Joan goes to church, then sends a warning message to the English.

When Joan and her men arrived to help the French troops, the English quickly surrendered the monastery and some even fled disguised as monks.

Confident of victory, she and her men chased the enemy to another English stronghold, a fortified monastery across the Loire River, and attacked them there. Joan injured her foot in the chase but was soon back with her men, who quickly overwhelmed the fort.

On 7 May, Joan and Count Jean attacked the besiegers around the city itself. Although wounded by an arrow, Joan continued to urge on her troops in the thick of the battle. The following day, as the French took control of both sides of the river, the invaders marched away from the city. Joan had won. She ordered her men not to attack the retreating English because it was Sunday.

## A miraculous wound

Several things that happened to Joan seemed to be miraculous, and made people think she was sent by God. When she was hit by an arrow at Orléans, it entered her body at exactly the point she had previously predicted, above her left breast. This was later used as part of the evidence that the church should make her a saint.

Below: Joan, holding her banner, announces the victory at Orléans to Charles. In this 15th-century image, the event is shown taking place at Loches Castle, by the Loire River.

**7 May 1429**
The French take further English fortifications around the city: victory is assured.

**8 May 1429**
The English lift the siege of Orléans and retreat. Joan has taken the city.

# Coronation

Saving the city of Orléans from the English was a huge triumph for Joan. She followed it with another victory at the town of Patay, where the English suffered more than 2,000 casualties but the French lost only three men. Several other towns on the Loire were also won by the French.

Despite her victories, Joan was shocked at the violence of war. She did not like to kill people herself, and usually went into battle carrying her banner to lead her troops, rather than brandishing her sword. But she knew that the bloodshed was necessary if she was to free her country from foreign rule and place Charles the Dauphin on the throne of France.

Charles, Joan and thousands of her men prepared to march toward Rheims, the city where French kings were traditionally crowned, for Charles's coronation. The coronation would show that Charles was ruler of his own country. It would also make it clear that the church was on his side, because the ceremony was a religious one and took place in the cathedral at Rheims.

Above: Rheims cathedral, the scene of the coronation, is one of the great medieval churches of France. It is famous for its tall stone arches, high vaulted ceiling and glowing stained-glass windows.

**11–18 June 1429**
There are further French attacks on Jargeau, Meung-sur-Loire, Beaugency and Patay.

**10 July 1429**
Joan and Charles enter the city of Troyes, whose inhabitants have agreed to receive Charles as their sovereign.

## A sacred ceremony

Medieval kings were powerful because of their wealth, and also because they had the backing of the church. Being a king was a sacred job as well as a worldly one, and it was important that every king was crowned in a church. During the coronation, the king was anointed (rubbed with holy oils) as a sign that the church blessed his reign.

Charles himself was worried, because, having already spent much of his money on the war, he had none left to pay all his soldiers and no supplies to feed them. But in the summer of 1429, this vast force, perhaps as many as 12,000 men, marched through France, gaining support and being given food as they went.

They arrived outside Rheims on 16 July 1429. A group of prominent citizens came out to meet them and offered Charles their obedience. The following day, Charles and his court entered the cathedral and, with Joan at his side, he was crowned. He was now king of France.

Joan was overwhelmed. She knelt in front of Charles, wept and embraced him. She was triumphant that she had played a major part in making him king. She was also relieved that their English enemies were on the retreat.

She did not pause to think about what her role would be now that she had achieved her goal.

**Left: Regnault de Chartres, Archbishop of Rheims, places the crown on Charles's head at the climax of the coronation ceremony.**

## 16 July 1429
The royal party arrives at Rheims, where they prepare for the coronation.

## 17 July 1429
Charles is anointed and crowned king in the cathedral at Rheims.

# Trouble Ahead

Once Charles was crowned king of France, Joan hoped he would go on and score further victories. She desperately wanted to take Paris, which was still held by the English, and drive their enemies out of France. But Charles and his royal advisers did not want any more battles.

Charles did not think that more fighting was really necessary. He was king now, and that was what mattered. In addition, his advisers, especially politician Georges de la Trémoille, reminded him that the royal funds were running low. They did not have much money left to pay for war. De la Trémoille, who looked after Charles's household and finances, took a strong dislike to Joan. He did not like the idea that a peasant girl might have influence over the king.

So Charles started to negotiate peace with the Burgundians. A treaty was drawn up, but Joan was suspicious of the deal – and the English still held large parts of France. So Joan and her loyal followers fought on. They marched through the region around Paris in an attempt to win this important area for Charles, and even tried to attack the capital itself. Joan was wounded again, in her thigh. After two days, Charles called off the attack.

## Paying for the army

In the Middle Ages, many fought because of their obligations to their lord. But kings also hired mercenaries, soldiers who fought for money, and all armies had to be equipped and fed, whether they were paid or not. By Joan's time, France and England had been at war for years, and both sides were having trouble finding the money needed.

**8 September 1429**
The French forces launch an attack on Paris, but after two days, Charles calls them back.

**November 1429**
The French besiege La Charité. The siege lasts almost until Christmas before it is abandoned.

In November 1429, however, Charles changed his mind and gave his authority for Joan to besiege the town of La Charité on the border with Burgundy. The siege was long and difficult, and Charles's support came with problems. He sent an army of mercenaries, or paid soldiers, to help Joan, but did not pay them. Their support was half-hearted and the siege was a failure.

Joan did have some success. When she marched to the town of Melun to the south of Paris, the people gave up their allegiance to Burgundy and declared themselves loyal subjects of Charles. But a shadow was cast over this triumph. Joan heard from her voices, who told her that by the summer of 1430 she would be taken prisoner. Since Joan believed everything the voices told her was true, this must have been the most devastating blow of all.

Below: In September 1429, the French attacked Paris. Joan was in the middle of the fighting, leading the assault on the English, who held onto the city.

**January 1430**
Joan is back at Orléans. She waits for reinforcements to be sent, but they do not arrive.

**March–April 1430**
Joan travels around the area to the northeast of Paris, hoping for support from Charles.

# Captured

By May 1430, things looked bad for Joan. She arrived at the town of Soissons, not far from Rheims, to find the Burgundians about to attack it. Joan wanted to cross the river to fight the Burgundians and save the town for the French. But the French captain of Soissons had other ideas. A traitor, he decided to sell his town to the Burgundians.

Joan and her army were disheartened by the captain's treachery. They were left camping in a field by the river, uncomfortable and hungry. Joan had no food left for her troops and the next morning most of them deserted her. Only two or three hundred men stayed loyal. But Joan refused to give up. She decided to come to the aid of another of the cities around Paris, Compiègne.

Above: When a ransom was paid in money, coins like these 14th-century French examples would change hands.

Joan and her small band of followers rode through the night to Compiègne. Joan thought that if they travelled quickly they would be able to take the Burgundians by surprise. At first she was successful. Because they were not expecting the attack, Joan was able to make several assaults on the Burgundian positions. But then Burgundian reinforcements and an English army arrived. The odds against Joan were now overwhelming. Realising that she was outnumbered, Joan tried to retreat to save her men.

## 15 May 1430
Joan is in the town of Compiègne, on the Oise River. She hopes to take the town from the Burgundians.

## 17 May 1430
Joan withdraws to Crépy-en-Valois, to the south of Compiègne, still hoping for reinforcements.

But the English cut off Joan's path and trapped her. She was stuck in a stretch of boggy ground outside the town, with no chance of either escaping or getting back inside the city to join her French friends. Then an enemy archer grabbed Joan, pulled her from her horse and took her prisoner. The archer handed her over to the Burgundian captain Jean de Luxembourg, who sent her to the fortress at Beaulieu, where she was imprisoned in a cell. She must have wondered whether Charles would come to her rescue.

## Knights and ransoms

Joan was in a strange position. Her brothers had both been made knights. Joan had her own heralds, indicating that she, too, was an important person on the battlefield. But she was a woman, and so could not be a knight. If she had been a man, her allies would certainly have paid her captors ransom money so that they would let her go. As a woman military leader, her future was uncertain.

Left: Philip the Good (reigned 1419–67) was ruler of Burgundy when Joan was captured. A few years after Joan's death he made peace with France. Burgundy eventually became part of France in 1477.

**22 May 1430**
Back outside Compiègne, Joan attacks.

**23 May 1430**
Joan is trapped in difficult countryside and captured by the Burgundians.

# PRISONER AND
# MARTYR

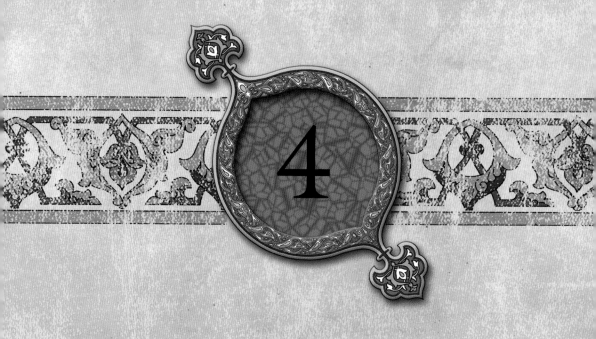

# In Prison

Usually when a knight or military commander was taken prisoner in the Middle Ages, he gave his word not to try to escape. But Joan was different. She had always believed that she had been obeying God's commands. So when she was put in prison, her first instinct was to carry on obeying God's orders and to escape, so that she could carry on the fight.

Her first escape attempt came soon after she was taken prisoner, when she tried unsuccessfully to take up the floorboards of her cell. She was moved to another prison, in John of Luxembourg's castle at Beaurevoir, where she jumped out of a window. The fall knocked her unconscious and she was recaptured.

Joan had female company at Beaurevoir, where three relatives of John of Luxembourg, also called Joan, had their home. As an important prisoner, Joan would have been allowed to talk to them and perhaps even take her meals with them.

The English wanted to get hold of Joan because she was clearly an inspirational figure for the French.

**Previous page: This statue of Joan on horseback now stands in Paris, the capital of a united France.**

**Left: The poor treatment that Joan received in captivity is shown in this sculpture of her captors mocking her while she was in prison.**

**27 May 1430**
Joan is held prisoner at Beaulieu, north of Compiègne.

**11 July 1430**
Joan begins a period of around four months' imprisonment in John of Luxembourg's tower at Beaurevoir.

**Right:** The Earl of Warwick, one of the English leaders, takes part in a tournament against an Italian knight in this late 15th-century drawing. Warwick, on the left, can be identified by his crest, a bear, on his helmet.

Some of the English leaders, including the Earl of Warwick, thought that if they could take Joan into custody, they would be able to convict her of some religious crime, perhaps proving that her voices came from the devil. If she was found guilty, Joan would be put to death, and the English would be rid of their enemy for good. So they paid John of Luxembourg a huge sum of money to hand over his prisoner to them.

Things were tough for Joan with the English. Her male jailers continuously taunted her. She insisted on wearing men's clothing because she felt that protected her much better from assaults than if she had worn a woman's dress. Joan was sent from one English stronghold to another, until, after eight months in jail, she arrived in Rouen. Here her trial was to be held.

## Imprisonment

In the 15th century, it was quite unusual for people to be kept in prison for long. Criminals were usually fined or beaten – or quickly executed if they had committed a serious offence. Prisoners of war could be exchanged. But Joan's case was different. She was a powerful leader for the French, and keeping her away from the battlefield was to the advantage of the English.

### November 1430
Joan leaves Beaurevoir and is taken on a long journey across northern France, eventually heading toward Rouen.

### 30 December 1430
Joan arrives at Rouen, where her trial will be held.

# The Medieval Church

In the Middle Ages, the church was at the centre of everyone's life. The church also played a large part in politics and held huge power. One reason for this was that priests and monks were among the few people who could read and write, so they often acted as ministers, ambassadors and advisors to kings. But in the 14th and 15th centuries, some people began to question the power of the church, saying that everyone should be able to understand the Bible without having a priest to interpret it for them. These reformers wanted a more direct relationship with God than that provided by the Catholic Church, and this made some churchmen suspicious of people like Joan, who claimed to hear saintly voices.

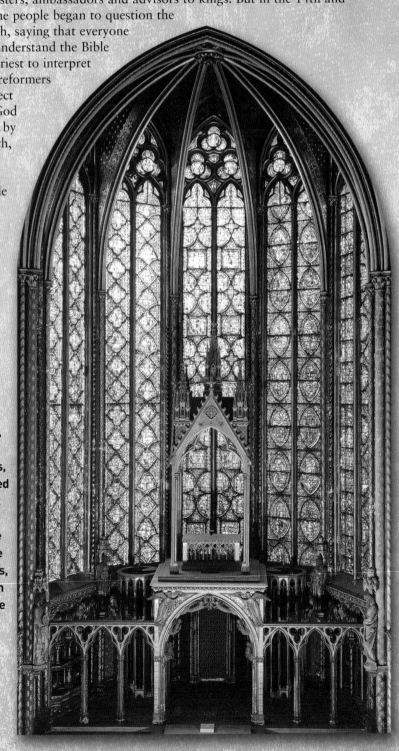

**Right: Great churches were the most magnificent buildings in Europe, decorated with beautiful sculptures, paintings and stained glass. The grandest churches, like the 13th-century Sainte Chapelle (right), the royal chapel in Paris, were built with such care because people believed that the proper worship of God was the most important of all human activities.**

Below: Medieval people felt that the end of the world was close, when God would send good people to heaven and sinners to hell. This 14th-century tapestry shows the devils that people thought lived in hell, based on the Book of Revelations in the Bible.

Left: The great Czech churchman Jan Hus (c. 1370–1415) was one of those who began to question the power of the Catholic Church. Like Joan, he was burned at the stake for his beliefs.

Right: The Catholic Church was so deeply divided in the late 14th and early 15th centuries that more than one pope ruled at the same time, one from Avignon in France, and another from Rome. This split was the result of arguments between churchmen and was known as the Great Schism. The Schism came to an end with the election of Pope Martin V (in the centre, crowned) in 1417, after which all popes ruled from Rome.

# The Trial

The English wanted to be rid of Joan. She was a powerful and daring military leader who had already scored several victories over them and helped to put a French king on the throne again. With her bravery, her striking grey horse and her banner waving in the wind, she was also a powerful symbol. The English were afraid that, if she was freed, thousands of French would gather around her once more.

So the English hatched a plan to bring Joan to trial in a church court – making sure that her judges were so biased against her that she would be sure to be sentenced to death. A powerful group of judges and prosecutors began to gather in Rouen to prepare to try Joan. Chief among them was Pierre Cauchon, Bishop of Beauvais and a powerful member of a group of churchmen based in Paris who were firmly on the side of England and Burgundy. Another was Jean d'Estivet, a colleague of Cauchon's, who was appointed 'promoter', or prosecutor, for the trial. By the time the trial began, an awe-inspiring group of bishops, priests and churchmen – all sympathetic to Cauchon – had grouped together to sit in judgment on Joan.

Above: A 15th-century manuscript about the events of the time of Charles VII shows a picture of Pierre Cauchon (right), judge at Joan's trial. He stands beside his clerk, Jean Massieu.

**9 January 1431**
The trial begins with investigations into Joan's past at Domrémy.

**13 January 1431**
The investigators read all the information about Joan that has been gathered and begin to plan their case.

Right: This panel of stained glass shows Joan wielding her sword and dressed in her armour. This was the kind of male dress that so offended the powerful churchmen who presided over her trial.

Since this was a church court, the charges against Joan were all to do with religion. She was accused of a number of different offences against the church – that she was a heretic (someone with religious beliefs that contradicted those of the church), that she practised witchcraft and that she was guilty of idolatry.

Idolatry could mean almost anything that Joan's judges wanted. In the Bible, people who worshipped 'idols', or false gods, were condemned. Joan's enemies accused her of idolatry because her voices could be those of false gods. But the accusers also singled out other things she did as being against the views of the church, such as wearing men's clothes. If the church was going to accuse her of wearing men's clothes, Joan realised she was going to have a difficult time proving herself innocent, since everyone had seen her wearing the armour of a soldier.

## The threat of heresy

The church was worried about heresy because it threatened its authority. Many people interpreted the Bible in different ways from the church. Some, like the Englishman John Wycliffe, said that the Bible itself was more important than what the clergy said about it. These threats to their authority made the bishops punish anyone with heretical beliefs severely.

## 21 February 1431

The first public session of the trial begins, and Joan is presented to the court.

## 10 March 1431

The prosecutors begin to try Joan in the prison rather than in public.

Above: People in the Middle Ages often accused those with unusual religious beliefs of witchcraft. These broomstick-riding witches are drawn in the margin of a book from the 15th century.

Every day in the courtroom, Joan's accusers questioned her about her beliefs about the voices, her religious views, her life as a soldier and her dressing in men's clothes. Although the questions were continuous and aggressive, and there was no one in court to defend her, Joan usually answered clearly. She insisted that the voices were those of the saints and that she only acted on God's command. She told her judges that she continued to wear men's clothes because she was frightened of being molested in prison by her male guards. She also reminded the court that Charles and the priests who tested her at Poitiers had found her to be good and sincere.

At first, Joan stood up well to her accusers. She insisted that she was as good a Christian as anyone else in court. And when Cauchon tried to taunt her, she got him back, saying that she knew things about him that she was not going to tell the court straight away. It was extraordinary – and dangerous – for Joan to turn on her powerful accuser in this way. She never carried out her threat.

## 9 May 1431
In the great tower of the castle at Rouen, Joan is threatened with torture.

## 13 May 1431
Several of Joan's English captors go to see her in her cell and try to persuade her to reject her heresy.

However, after days of questioning and weeks spent in chains in prison threatened with violence, Joan began to break down. Things became worse when Cauchon began to question her in her cell rather than the court. She saw few people who were sympathetic to her, apart from her confessor, a friar called Martin Ladvenu. The court called none of Joan's friends or family as witnesses.

Finally, after being shown torture instruments and being falsely promised that she would be taken to a church prison under the care of women, Joan signed a confession saying that her voices did not come from God. However, realising she had been frightened and tricked, she took back her confession almost immediately.

## The confessor

Members of the Catholic Church are expected to confess their sins regularly to a priest, and to perform any penance (punishment) that this priest, or 'confessor', hands out. The confessor is not allowed to tell anyone what he is told during confession. In the Middle Ages, people were usually very close to their confessors and this seems to have been true of Joan and the friar Martin Ladvenu.

Right: This example of Joan's signature comes from a letter she wrote to Jean, Count of Dunois. She would have signed her confession in a similar way, with just her first name, in the fashion of the time.

**23 May 1431**
A full explanation of all the charges is read out to Joan.

**24 May 1431**
Joan signs the document denying her views, but then changes her mind.

# Burned at the Stake

By now it was clear that no one would be able to make Joan change her mind. She was still convinced that she had acted according to God's commands and that she had done nothing wrong. The English, increasingly frustrated by the months taken over Joan's questioning and trial, were eager for her death.

And so the churchmen who had tried Joan delivered their verdict – that she should be handed back to her English captors as a guilty woman. The churchmen knew that the English would execute her. The usual form of execution for heretics in the Middle Ages was by burning, and Joan was to be burned in the marketplace of Rouen.

**Above: An illustration shows Joan at Rouen in her final moments of life, waiting at the stake before her captors lit a fire at her feet.**

For much of the time of her trial Joan's prosecutors had forbidden her to go to church to receive Holy Communion. In other words, she had been excommunicated, or cut off from the church. Medieval Christians believed that someone who had been excommunicated and could not have their last confession heard by a priest, would not be able to go to heaven.

## 28 May 1431
Joan is sent back to prison, charged with being a relapsed heretic.

## 29 May 1431
Joan's prosecutors and the other members of the court have a meeting to decide what to do about Joan.

Right: A crucifix like this 15th-century one was held in front of Joan as the flames took her life. The image of Jesus on the cross would have given her courage as she perished.

At the last minute, Cauchon changed his mind and Joan was allowed to receive Holy Communion. The friar Martin Ladvenu was sent to hear her last confession. Joan was now prepared for death.

On 30 May 1431, Joan was led barefoot through the streets of Rouen. She bowed her head, so that she did not have to look at anyone, and was able to control her emotions until she saw the stake where she was about to be burned. Then she burst into tears. As they tied her to the stake, Joan asked for a cross to be held in front of her. An English soldier held two sticks together in the form of a cross, but then someone ran into the nearby church of St Saveur and brought back a crucifix. As Joan died, the last image before her eyes was of Jesus on the cross, and she called out Jesus' name several times as the flames engulfed her. One bystander, John Tressart, the English king's secretary, said, 'We are lost; we have burned a saint.'

## Methods of execution

There were many methods of execution in the Middle Ages. Upper-class people were beheaded – this was the least painful method available. Poorer people were hanged. The most painful was burning, which was for those who had committed religious crimes.

**30 May 1431**
Joan is burned at the stake in the marketplace at Rouen.

**June 1431**
The controversy about Joan's life begins, when some people declare that she was an innocent martyr.

# Changing their Minds

Many French people were uncomfortable with the way in which the English authorities, together with a section of the church, had been able to put Joan to death. Nothing could bring Joan back, but they could do something to set the record straight.

By the 1450s, a lot had changed in Europe. There was a new pope, Nicholas V, who was no friend of the Parisian clergy who had run Joan's trial. Charles was still on the French throne and he was stronger, winning a number of battles to take most of his kingdom back from the English. And, in 1455, the church mounted an official investigation into Joan's trial and death.

**Left: Many of the pictures of Joan made after her lifetime try to portray several sides of her character. In this 19th-century statue, her sword indicates that she was a military leader, the banner stands for her religious beliefs, and the French fleur-de-lis pattern on her clothes reminds us that she fought for her king and country.**

Jehanne an Sacre

## 1449
Charles VII asks the pope, Nicholas V, to authorise a new trial to examine the evidence against Joan.

## 17 November 1455
The 'retrial' opens, with Guillaume d'Estouteville, cousin of Charles VII, in charge.

The investigation was like a trial without a prisoner. The judges called many witnesses, this time speaking to people who were sympathetic to Joan. They began by calling Joan's mother and then questioned people from Domrémy. These witnesses had not been allowed to speak at Joan's original trial. The judges concluded that Joan was a sincere, pious person, and that the voices must have been authentic. They also recognised that she had been unfairly treated – for example, that she should have been held in a church prison. They also said that she had been treated badly by the churchmen, who must have realised their mistake, otherwise they would not have allowed her to receive Holy Communion before she died.

Whereas in the first trial the judges were biased against Joan, this new group of judges went out of their way to be sympathetic to her. They did not ask any probing questions about the precise source of the voices she heard, and they did not examine the issue of Joan's male clothes, which had been such a problem in the original trial. But their conclusions were far fairer than those of the original trial, and their estimate of her character, as a loyal and sincere Christian woman, was accurate. The people agreed. Statues of Joan started to appear in French towns, and she was soon seen as a national hero.

## Martyrs of the church

A martyr is someone who is killed because of their beliefs. Since the earliest times, Christians had been attacked, and some of the first saints were people who had lost their lives through religious persecution. When the judges at the retrial ruled that Joan had been wrongly executed, she was seen as a martyr, and won the respect of churchmen and pious Christians.

### December 1455–March 1456
The judges order investigations in several of the towns associated with Joan – Rouen, Domrémy and Orléans.

### 7 July 1456
The retrial ends, with the decision that Joan was wrongly executed.

# Joan's Legacy

By the time the retrial was over, Joan was a French hero. She was a country girl who had, by inspiring those around her, saved her land from foreign rule. As such, she became a key figure in the national image of France, and her statue is seen in many places, especially in cities associated with her, such as Rouen.

Authors became fascinated by Joan, because she was such a powerful personality and so different from the people around her. Many were astonished that she did not do what was expected of a woman in the 15th century – she did not play the usual role of wife and mother and she had an influence that was unique for a member of her social class. All this made her a good subject for dramatists, and

Above: Victorian painters saw Joan as a Romantic heroine. The 19th-century British painter Dante Gabriel Rossetti painted her lifting her sword while looking upward, as if toward God.

Joan features in plays by the German writer Friedrich Schiller, the French dramatist Jean Anouilh and the Irish playwright George Bernard Shaw.

## 1801

Friedrich Schiller produces *The Maid of Orléans*, the first drama in which Joan is the main character.

## 1845

*Giovanna d'Arco*, an opera about Joan by composer Giuseppe Verdi, premieres in Italy.

Poets wrote about her, and many artists painted her picture, in spite of the fact that no one knows what she really looked like.

The church also took a great interest in Joan's life and character. In the 19th century, a movement began to get her recognised as a saint. In the Catholic Church, this is a long process, involving investigation and debate about the life of the candidate for sainthood, and evidence about miracles performed by the person, which are said to be proof of their holiness. In Joan's case, the process took about 50 years, and she was finally declared a saint of the Catholic Church in 1920.

Joan also became a hero to women. She stood out in the Middle Ages because she showed that women could play an important part in affairs of state and warfare, areas which in this period were dominated by men. But her willingness to challenge the authorities, to question normal ideas and fashions, and to take the lead at a time when women were expected to follow their men, has been an inspiration to women in later centuries, too.

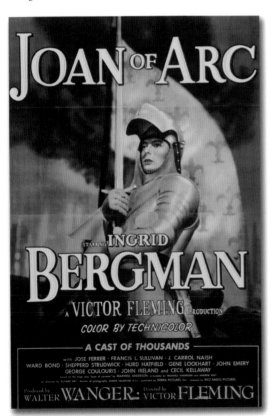

**Left: Victor Fleming's 1948 film, *Joan of Arc*, featured Ingrid Bergman in the title role. The actress, although too old to play a teenager, managed to portray Joan's strong, idealistic views.**

### 1920
The Catholic Church declares Joan to be a saint.

### 1928
*The Passion of Joan of Arc*, the first feature film about Joan, is released in France.

# Glossary

**abbess** woman who is the head of a nunnery.

**anointed** rubbed with holy oils; a person is anointed as part of a ceremony such as a coronation, as a sign that the person is given the blessing of God and the church.

**battering ram** device consisting of a wooden beam or tree trunk supported on some kind of framework, used for battering down the gate or door of a castle or city wall.

**booty** valuable articles obtained through plunder, especially during war.

**Burgundy** area in east-central France, now part of France itself but in Joan of Arc's time a separate state ruled by a duke.

**cavalrymen** the unit of an army composed of troops on horseback.

**coat of arms** symbolic design painted on a shield or worn on clothing, used to identify members of specific noble or royal families.

**confessor** priest who listens to people when they confess their sins.

**court** group of people, mainly of noble birth, who advised and attended to a medieval king.

**crest** badge or design forming the topmost part of a coat of arms and sometimes worn on soldiers' helmets to show on whose side they were fighting.

**dauphin** eldest surviving son of the king of France and so heir to the French throne.

**devout** deeply religious.

**duchy** the territory ruled by a duke or duchess.

**excommunication** the process of banning someone from the church, especially from the rite of Holy Communion.

**fortified** strengthened against attack, such as by building high walls.

**herald** person who acted as the messenger of a knight, nobleman or monarch, who organised ceremonies, and who was in charge of the design of coats of arms.

**heretic** person who holds religious beliefs that differ from those of the church.

**Holy Communion** the most important rite of the Christian church, in which people take bread and wine that has been blessed and represents the body and blood of Christ.

**Hundred Years' War** conflict between France and England that lasted from 1337 to 1453, although fighting was not continuous throughout this period.

**idolatry** literally, the worship of statues or images, but the word was used in the Middle Ages to refer to any belief in what the Catholic Church considered to be false gods or false prophets.

**illegitimate** a child born to parents who were not married to each other.

**illumination** the decoration of a manuscript or book with pictures and designs.

**knight** a man who did military service for his lord.

**longbow** a bow drawn by hand and usually similar in length to the height of a man. Longbows were distinct from crossbows, which were drawn with a mechanical device.

**lord** a titled nobleman, such as a count or duke, who held land from the king. A lord allowed peasants to farm most of his land in return for a share of the crops they produced. The lord offered his king loyalty and military help in times of war.

**man-at-arms** medieval soldier who usually fought on foot and was lower in rank than a knight.

**medieval** referring to the Middle Ages, the period extending roughly from 500 to 1500.

**mercenary** soldier who fought in return for money, rather than as part of the service that was due to his lord.

**noble** a person having a title or rank, such as duke or count, that passed down from father to son.

**page** boy who worked as a servant in a royal or noble household, often as part of his training to become a knight.

**peasant** farmer who paid rent to his lord in the form of produce or services.

**penance** punishment, usually imposed by a priest, to show that the person is sorry for the sins they have committed.

**pilgrimage** journey, usually over a long distance, to visit a church or other holy place.

**pious** deeply religious and moral.

**prophecy** prediction, or foretelling, of some future event.

**prosecutor** person who presents the case against the accused in a court of law.

**ransom** money paid to buy the release of a prisoner.

**reformer** person who works to bring about improvements, especially in the church.

**relapsed** slipped back, particularly into wrongdoing.

**saint** in the Catholic Church, a person officially recognised as having lived a holy life.

**schism** split as the result of a difference of opinion, especially in the church.

**scribe** person whose job involved writing and copying documents or books.

**shrine** place where holy relics – such as the body of a saint or objects relating to a saint – are kept.

**siege** method of warfare used against a castle or town, in which an enemy surrounded the castle and attempted to take it over.

**standard** flag or banner on a pole, carried into battle to identify a specific commander or fighting force.

**steward** person who managed the household of a monarch, nobleman or knight.

**Testament** one of the two parts of the Christian Bible: the Old Testament or the New Testament.

**tournament** sporting occasion of the Middle Ages at which knights gathered for mock battles and other military contests.

# Bibliography

*Beyond the Myth: The Story of Joan of Arc*, Brooks, Polly Schoyer, published by Lippincott, 1990

*Joan of Arc*, Gordon, Mary, published by Weidenfeld & Nicolson, 2000

*Joan of Arc*, Pernoud, Régine, published by Penguin, 1969

*Joan of Arc: A Military Leader*, DeVries, Kelly, published by Sutton Publishing, 1999

*Joan of Arc: Her Story*, Pernoud, Régine, and Clin, Marie-Véronique, published by Phoenix Press, 2000

*Medieval Children*, Orme, Nicholas, published by Yale University Press, 2001

*Saint Joan of Arc*, Sackville-West, Vita, published by Image Books, 1991

*Women in Medieval Life*, Labarge, Margaret Wade, published by Hamish Hamilton, 1986

Source of quote:

**p. 55** Sackville-West, Vita, *Saint Joan of Arc*, Image Books, 1991, p. 324

Some Web sites that will help you to explore Joan of Arc's world:

archive.joan-of-arc.org
Joan of Arc Archive: large collection of articles, documents, transcripts, details of Joan's trial and other information.

members.aol.com/TeacherNet/medieval.html
An educational reference site with links for all aspects of medieval history.

www.smu.edu/ijas
International Joan of Arc Society: extensive collection of texts, resources and links.

www.stjoan-center.com
St Joan of Arc Center: comprehensive site about Joan, with many links.

# Index

Agincourt, Battle of 11, 14–15
Arc, Catherine of (sister) 9
Arc, Isabelle of (mother) 8–11, 13, 57
Arc, Jacques of (father) 8–10
Arc, Jacques of (brother) 9, 11
Arc, Jean of (brother) 9, 11, 32
Arc, Joan of (Jeanne d'Arc) 8
  'Jeannette' 10
  attempts escape 46
  birth of 8–9
  burned at the stake 54–55
  captured 42–43
  childhood 10–11, 16
  confession of 53
  excommunication 54
  family 8–9
  hears voices of saints 18, 41
  martyr 55

  museum dedicated to life of 29
  religion 12–13, 18
  retrial 56
  sainthood 59
  sent to prepare for battle 27–29
  statues of 57
  sword of 28–29
  trial of 50–52
  victory at Orléans 37
  work 11
  wounded in battle 37, 40
Arc, Pierre of (brother) 9, 32
archers 34, 35
armour 28, 32, 51
Ascension Day 36
Aulon, Jean d' 32
Auxerre 15
Avignon 15, 49

banners 29
'Bastard of Orléans' *see* Jean, Count of Dunois
Baudricourt, Robert de 18, 22–23, 26
Beaugency 15, 38
Beaulieu-les-Fontaines 15, 43, 46
Beaurevoir 15, 46
Beauvais, Bishop of *see* Cauchon, Pierre
Bedford, John, Duke of 17
Bergman, Ingrid 59
Bermont 12
Bible, the 8, 48, 51
Bingen, Hildegard of 24
Blois 15, 32–33
booty 16
bows 17
Burgundy 15, 17, 41, 50

Burgundy Gate 32
Burgundy, Duke of 9, 12, 14

Catherine of France 13
Cauchon, Pierre, Bishop of
    Beauvais 50, 52–53, 55
Charles the Dauphin 16, 22,
    26–28, 32, 37–39
Charles V, King of France 25
Charles VI, King of France
    13–14, 16
Charles VII, King of France
    39–40, 50, 56
    *see also* Charles the Dauphin
Chécy 33
Chinon 15, 22–23, 26, 28–
    29
Chinon Castle 23, 26, 29
Christ 12, 27, 29, 55
church, the 11, 48–49, 53, 59
coats of arms 29
Compiègne 15, 42–43, 46
confessors 53
coronation 39
Crécy, Battle of 15
Crépy-en-Valois 15, 42
crossbows 17

Domrémy 8–10, 12, 15–19, 23,
    27, 50, 57
dragon 19

Edward III, King of England 8,
    14
England 8, 14–15
envoys 14
Estivet, Jean d' 50
Estouteville, Guillaume d'
    56
Eve 8
executions 47, 61

fairies 12
Fierbois 15
Fleming, Victor 59
    *Joan of Arc* 59
fleur-de-lis 15, 26, 56
Formigny 15
Fouquet, Jean 28

France 8–9, 14–17, 25
Franciscans 27
friars 27

games 11
Garonne 15
Gien 15
'Great Schism' 11, 49

Henry V, King of England 10,
    12–14, 16–17
Henry VI, King of England
    22
heralds 32
heresy 51–52
Hundred Years' War 8, 14–16
Hus, Jan 10, 49

idolatry 51
Italy 15

Jargeau 38
Jean, Count of Dunois 32–33,
    36–37, 53

La Charité 15, 40–41
Ladvenu, Martin 53, 55
Last Judgment, the 49
lions of England 15
Loire River 15, 28, 32, 37–
    38
London 15
longbows 17
Luxembourg, Jean de 43, 46–47

Martin V, Pope 11, 49
Massieu, Jean 50
medicine 13, 36
Melun 15, 41
men-at-arms 16–17, 29
mercenaries 40–41
Meung-sur-Loire 38
Meuse 15
Middle Ages, the 9, 18
mining 35

Neufchâteau 15, 19
Nicholas V, Pope 56
Normandy 12, 15

Notre Dame de la Grande at
    Poitiers, Church of 26
nuns 25

Oise River 15, 42
Orléans 15, 32–33, 36–38, 41,
    57
Orléans, dukes of 9, 32

Paris 15, 40–41, 46, 50
Patay 15, 38
Philip IV, King of France 8,
    14
Philip the Good 12, 43
pilgrimage 8
Pisan, Christine de 25
Poitiers 15, 26–27, 52
priests, role of 13, 19, 48
prison 46–47, 53
'promoter' 50

raiders 16–17
ransoms 42, 43
Regnault de Chartes,
    Archbishop of Rheims
    39
Revelations, Book of 49
Rheims 15, 38–39, 42
Rheims Cathedral 38–39
Rhône River 15
Rome 49
Rossetti, Dante Gabriel 58
Rouen 15, 47, 50, 52, 54–55,
    57

St Catherine 18–19
St Catherine at Fierbois, Church
    of 28
St Denis 15
St Francis of Assisi 27
St Loup, Monastery of 36
St Margaret 18–19
St Michael 18–19
Sainte Chapelle, Paris 48
saints 12, 18–19, 57, 59
Satan 19
Schiller, Friedrich 58
    *The Maid of Orléans* 58
seals 32

Seine River 15
Shaw, George Bernard 58
sieges 32, 33, 34, 35, 36, 37, 40,
    41
siege towers 34
Soissons 15, 42
Soissons, Captain of 42
Somme 15
spinning 24
stained glass 38, 48, 51
standards 28–29
Switzerland 15

tapestry 23
Thames River 15
torture instruments 53
Tours 15, 28–29, 32
toys 11
trebuchets 35
Trémoille, Georges de la 40
Tressart, John 55
Troyes 15, 38
Troyes, Treaty of 13

Vaucouleurs 15, 22
Verdi, Giuseppe 58

Giovanna d'Arco 58
Vienne River 15
Virgin Mary 12
voices 18–19

walled cities 32
warfare 14, 15, 34, 35
Warwick, Earl of 46–47
witchcraft 52
women 11, 13, 24–25, 27, 43,
    58, 59
wooden houses 33
Wycliffe, John 51

# Acknowledgments

Sources: AA = Art Archive, AKG = akg-images

B = bottom, C = centre, T = top

**Front cover:** AKG/Erich Lessing.

**Pages: 3–8** AKG; **9** AA/Dagli Orti; **10** AA/Musée Conde Chantilly/Dagli Orti; **13** AKG/Chantilly Musée Conde; **14T&B** Scala, Florence/HIP; **15** AA/Bibliothèque Nationale, Paris; **16–17** Scala, Florence/HIP; **18** Scala, Florence; **19T** AKG/British Library; **19B** The Stained Glass Museum, Ely Cathedral; **21** AKG/Erich Lessing; **22** AKG/Herve Champollion; **23** AA; **24C&B** AKG; **25T** Bridgeman Art Library; **25B** AKG/British Library; **26** John Parker; **27** Bridgeman Art Library; **28** AA/Musee du Louvre Paris/Dagli Orti (A); **29** AKG/Herve Champollion; **31** AA/Archives Nationales Paris/Marc Charmet; **32** AA/Centre Jeanne d'Arc, Orleans/Dagli Orti; **33** AA/Dagli Orti; **34C** AA/JFB; **34B** AA/Bibliothèque Nationale, Paris; **35T&B** Scala, Florence/HIP; **36** AKG; **37** Bridgeman Art Library; **38** John Parker; **39** AKG/Jerome da Cunha; **41** AKG/Bibliothèque Nationale, Paris; **42** AKG/CDA/Guillemot; **43** Scala, Florence/HIP; **45** Corbis/Nik Wheerler; **46** Corbis/Alan Towse/Ecoscene; **47** AKG/Herve Champollion; **48** AKG/Erich Lessing; **49T** John Parker; **49C** AKG; **49B** Scala, Florence; **50** AKG/Jerome da Cunha; **51** Corbis/Dave Bartruff; **52** AKG/Bibliothèque Nationale, Paris; **53** AA/Centre Jeanne d'Arc, Orleans/Dagli Orti; **54** AKG/Jerome da Cunha; **55** AKG; **56** AKG/Alfons Rath; **58** Corbis/Christie's Images; **59** Corbis/CinemaPhoto.